31. PLENTY OF POEMS ARE POMPOUS

32. 14's A HORRIBLE AGE

33. CAR MECHANICS

34. OBAMA

35. QUIZ CHEATS

36. THEN THE ALARM CLOCK WENT OFF

37. HOME TOWN

38. WHAT'S IT LIKE BEING PERFECT?

39. WHEN I WERE A LAD (2046 A.D.)

40. TAKING UP SPACE AT THE BAR

41. HEROES OF '66

42. FIRST JOB

43. THE TIMES NEWSPAPER

44. INSURANCE CLAIMS

45. NORTHERN SOUL

46. IF

47. WHERE DO SINGLE SOCKS GO?

48. WE'VE BEEN DRAWN AWAY TO NEPTUNE (3046 A.D.)

49. COWELL

50. STOKE-ON-TRENT

IMAGE CREDITS

Used with permission from Microsoft.

All images found by searching : http://office.microsoft.com/en-us/images

Thank you once more for spending a few hard-earned pennies or
cents on this edition. Also a HUGE thank you to those who
purchased my first effort.

'50 Silly Poems from Modern England'

Available in Kindle e-book or paperback format from
www.amazon.com or www.amazon.co.uk

CONTENTS

1. MANCHESTER
2. CHRISTMAS
3. OUT-OF-TOWN-SHOPS
4. FRIENDS' PARENTS
5. 1970's BEDROOM
6. NO-ONE TALKS (MUCH) ANYMORE
7. DAD'S GENERATION
8. PAUL
9. FOOTBALL MANAGER
10. RUFF TALK POSH, POSH TALK RUFF
11. GIRLS LUV CHOCOLATE
12. BOYS LUV BEER
13. DAVID CASSIDY
14. SUNGLASSES
15. BLACKPOOL
16. PANTOMIMES
17. COFFEE
18. THE OLD DON'T RATE THE YOUNG
19. ROAD RAGE
20. HAIR DYE
21. GOLF
22. WE'RE RUBBISH AT FOREIGN LANGUAGES
23. MEN AT FOOTBALL MATCHES
24. DON'T SPOIL THE SHIP
25. RAMSAY
26. AUDIENCE IN AN ARENA
27. CRICKET
28. MOVE YER MONEY ABOUT
29. HOMES
30. FUNERALS

1. MANCHESTER

In the North of England there's a place which

For two centuries plus punched above it's weight

Manchester, birthplace of industrialisation

For the developed World, became the template

Mechanisation, engineering know – how

Imports, exports, building projects so vast

The World watched and then copied

The original prototype had been cast

It's produced Alan Turing, computers pioneer

The artist Lowry and his matchstick men

Stone Roses, Happy Mondays, the Smiths, New Order

A football club which wins the league time and again

Davy Jones from The Monkees was a 'Manc'

The Bee Gees too, the actor Ian McShane

The ship canal was a direct link with America

They also had the first station for a passenger train

It's politics have always leaned to the left

Even Karl Marx lived here for a while

Emmaline Pankhurst, the Peterloo massacre

But now there's plenty to bring a smile

The presenter Terry Christian always promotes MCR

There's comedians such as Jason Manford and Peter Kay

Caroline Aherne, singers Russell Watson, Elkie Brooks

Grew up in this habitat and often there still play

The 1996 bomb rocked Manchester

Marks and Spencer's was laid flat

But it rose again, re-built, from the ashes

With Simply Red, Oasis, Take That

Did I mention that Rolls first met Royce here ?

And London musicals are staged in the city

And as the Coronation Street cast tend to express

Mancunians : often bold as brass, sometimes gritty

2.   CHRISTMAS

Christmas .... a surreal time of year

Lots of blurred lines, nothing's clear

Those normally quiet suddenly full of cheer

Maybe spurred on by wine, spirits, beer

A time for giving, a time for sharing

A time to show you're capable of caring

A time to, perhaps, show you're daring

Whilst a Colin Firth pullover, you'll be wearing

Once the stove, by the matriarch, has been lit

People will claim they want to 'do their bit'

But for many the booze will prove a more popular hit

While others parade in and show off their new kit

Christmas, the fantasy of every marketing man

A self-fulfilling industry, more powerful than

Weddings and birthdays, a season that can

Turn non-believers into a baby Jesus 'fan'

3. OUT-OF-TOWN SHOPS

The city centre's dying

Shops are moving out-of-town

For them, sales figures are up

But for high street stores they're down

Free parking and other incentives

Are dangled in front of those who shop

The main roads all lead to the retail park

There's free buses on which you can hop

Everyone seems to have an urge

To escape from the good old city

And if you surround retail with a few trees

They'll claim it's eco-friendly – a pity

The same with sports stadiums, offices, hubs

All moved miles away to 're-locate'

The soul's been ripped out of the city

'cause the planners and developers have bitten the bait !

4. FRIENDS' PARENTS

When you're a certain formative age

You're embarrassed by your Mum and Dad

But strangely you view your friends' parents

As quite interesting, they're really "not bad"

Funny that a conversation with

Your folks is all "uhm" "yeah" "dunno"

But your friend's Mum shows interest

In you and the chat easily starts to flow

Your friend's Dad's interests appeal

As he goes to tennis or starts to jog

But your own Dad is turned down

When you're asked to join him and walk the dog

Your friend's Mum's cups of tea

Always appear to be warm and sweet

But if your own Mum wanted company

She'd need to hunt you first, street after street

5. 1970's BEDROOM

The 1970's bedroom for teenagers

An interesting place

Fungus-ridden, damp skirting boards

Nothing like today's 'modern space'

Posters of footballers and singers on walls

Dad wouldn't allow Page 3 girls

Flock wallpaper, nasty furniture

Threadbare carpet with flowery swirls

We'd moved from a one bedroom flat

To a three-bedroomed town house

Relatively clean and sound

No rodents, just the odd slug or woodlouse

The radiator did work occasionally

And the red lightbulb we thought was magic

But thinking back to the naivety and innocence

It was hardly exciting, just gloomily tragic

6. NO-ONE TALKS (MUCH) ANYMORE

Not many of us talk much in the West

It's easier to text, tweet or e-mail

No longer discreet private phone calls

Because laptops all leave a trail

I'm as bad as the next person

Online you connect when it suits you

No awkward excuses why you can't talk

No fake expression needed too

You can write at 6 a.m. or midnight

And it'll never be the 'wrong' time

You can write from any location

Often won't cost a penny or dime

There's still some chat in the workplace

And in cafe's, restaurants and bars

But once someone returns home alone

They might as well be living on Mars

7. DAD'S GENERATION

Our Dads were homophobic

They couldn't help it really

They were generally decent chaps

All willing to help....well, nearly

They'd take care of the family

In every possible way

Kids properly clothed and fed

Bills sorted out on pay-day

But Larry Grayson walks onto the telly

Dad goes in a huff

John Inman enters a scene it's,

"Look at that professional puff!"

They couldn't help it our Dads

Not allowed to show emotion or passion

Whether at Liberace or Boy George they'd yell

"Don't tell me that's bloody fashion!"

8. PAUL

I grew up with a lad named Paul

He was only 5 feet six, not exactly tall

Used to tell people he was my brother

Not sure why he chose me over any other

Showed disturbing traits through his action

Was he mentally ill? More than a fraction

Would take on anyone in a fight

Seeing an opponent in pain would bring delight

Hated authority and almost everyone

Where is he now? Deceased....... gone

Another user of amphetamine, speed

Those of you tempted, take heed

As a young lad, Paul was clean, healthy, fit

Then decided the everyday World was quite shit

Only thought the glossy, fast version was smart

Ultimately caused his body to fall apart

R.I.P.

9. FOOTBALL MANAGER

They know all about football

But many are not extremely bright

And in the 1970's they only

Had to speak on T.V. once a fortnight

But due to the global packaging

Of the sport on Sky T.V.

Poor manager Ron, Ted or Mario

Has to meet the media daily

It's difficult to know what to say

Should he moan about last night's referee

Or talk about the form of his defence

Or show concern at the latest injury

The media will present him as a comic

As a philosopher, a politician, a sage

But we know how limited his intellect is

And there's no way he earns <u>THAT</u> wage!

10. RUFF TALK POSH – POSH TALK RUFF

Isn't it extraordinary that

When someone moves out to 'the sticks'

They start to talk different 'cause it's

A cultured breed with which they now mix

For example, a person who

Used to reside in Salford or Longsight

On moving to Wilmslow or Alderley Edge will now

Speak politely when bidding you "goodnight"

They used to say 'grub' 'tea-time' or 'starters'

But now use gastro-phrases such as hors d'oeuvres

Or supper, canapés, aperitifs,

It might possibly get on your nerves

Conversely, the flip side of the coin

Will see someone RADA-trained at stage school

Reject the silver spoon placed in one's mouth

And think saying "innit" is cool

They'll use colloquialisms to stay 'relevant'

Finish sentences with "D'ya know what I mean?"

Brag about their edgy pad in the urban zone

But we know where you're from and where you've been

11. GIRLS LUV CHOCOLATE

Girls love chocolate

Nothing wrong with that

But the ever-so-tasty calories

Leaves 'em feeling 'fat'

It's a dilemma isn't it?

One which won't subside

That which makes us feel 'good'

Leaves us thinking it has also 'lied'

It's promoted as sensual and classy

It feels good and tastes good too

But the sugar and milk that's crammed into it

Sticks to the waist and hips like glue

Girls love chocolate

Would queue for the stuff all day long

Is it the sense of creamy luxury

Or is it that we know it's so 'wrong' ?

12. BOYS LUV BEER

Boys love beer

In cans in glasses in jars

They'll drink it in any vessel

In a range of pubs, clubs and bars

Very few could name the ingredients

Very few could explain the brew process

Very few acknowledge the dangers

Very few, when sick, clean up their mess

Particularly when far from home

Many will pay for one beer a silly price

It's a habit it's addictive it's sad

Just like smoking, I'm afraid it's a vice

But in moderation it can be fun

It can loosen inhibition, help you to chat

Just don't kid yourself it's <u>you</u> that's dynamic

The sugar converted to alcohol – it's that!

13. DAVID CASSIDY

The 1970's version of 'sex on legs'

In girls' eyes he could do no wrong

Shoulder-length hair, sparkling eyes

As he sang a romantic pop song

Was it that he looked vulnerable?

Was it his delicate smile?

Was it the trendy clothes he wore?

Or the way he made other men seem so vile?

He could sing he could dance he could act

In the T.V. soap Partridge Family

And as millions of girls watched in awe

Their knees would turn kind of trembly

He was a bit like a one-man One Direction

And for a period he was at the top of his game

But the motto 'everything is temporary'

Is one he must now face up to – a shame

14. SUNGLASSES

'D' List celebrities tend to

Wear sunglasses when indoors

Does it make them dynamic and brill

Or does it make them pathetic bores?

What are they thinking of?

Protecting their eyes from what?

Or is it their way of saying

Look who I am, look what I've got?

Sunglasses used to be a disguise

Worn by proper stars in the news

But these pretenders today, well,

No-one cares about their views

No-one's interested who you are

No-one's interested in your 'look' that's moody and mean

You can take those silly shades off now

So your ordinary-ness can be seen!

15. BLACKPOOL

One of the World's first sea-side towns

Where families would go for a holiday

England's biggest and most brash

For most entertainment, a modest fee you'll pay

Yes we know it's not the Riviera

The Costa del Sol or The Med

And it's not the Canaries or Florida and

You won't require a sunlounger or bed

But it has charm, has history and form

The oldest rollercoaster anywhere

And if you can't find something to amuse you

You really must be a snob, you're square

Fish and chips, piers, the Winter Gardens

A tower just like the one in Paris, France

A pleasure beach so huge it's daunting

Blackpool's worth more than a passing glance

16. PANTOMIMES

Tourists to England don't understand

The phenomenon that is pantomime

A strange beast which only rears it's head

Round about Christmas time

Men play the parts of ladies

Ladies play the parts of young boys

There's much frivolity and hilarity

Songs, fights and boisterous noise

Scenes from the old days form a backcloth

While fairy tales loosely form a plot

Some of the script is witty and humorous

Whether it makes sense – we don't care a jot

There's opportunities for dancing

The audience as well as the cast

Long live the traditional 'panto'

Don't let it become a 'thing of the past'

17. COFFEE

I wonder how much coffee

Mr. Average consumes in a day

Is it 2 cups 3 cups 4 cups?

Certainly helps keep fatigue at bay

But is it any good for you?

The jury seems to be out

Does it cause blood pressure to rise?

Does it cause your heart to pass out?

It has a reputation for

Being conversational and sophisticated

And is a wonderful antidote

For when you're extra-inebriated

Although beer and tea are OK

I love coffee, it's my number one drink

The smell of a rich, dark roast

Helps me to concentrate ....I think?

18. THE OLD DON'T RATE THE YOUNG

The old don't rate the young

Nothing good to say about 'em

If it was up to them national service would return

With a sergeant-major allowed to clout 'em

The oldsters' memories are certainly short

You'd think everyone was well-heeled in 1940

You'd think everyone was well-mannered, polite

You'd think no-one was ever naughty

Perhaps adultery, theft and deception

Only commenced in the last decade

As for drugs and alcohol-abuse

Have people only now, down this path, strayed?

I know it's tough to admit

And hard to face up to this fact

But for centuries people have been drunk

Have been robbing and have been attacked

19. ROAD RAGE

People on a short fuse on Fridays

Stare, shout and gesticulate

Why is it always a Friday

When people are stressed about meeting a mate?

What's the rush? Why the panic?

Is it really worth getting so tense?

What is this epic meeting you're due at?

Impress us, please, we're in suspense

Can't justify it, can you?

The screaming, the blood-pressure so high

The ridiculous temper, the violence

You say it's necessary? Such a lie

Come on, so the guy in front

Drives 5 m.p.h. slower than you

Does not give you the right

To behave like you belong in a zoo

20. HAIR DYE

Saw three hairs last night

With my very own eyes

I'll be straight down to the shops

To check out a range of hair dyes

I'm one of the first in my circle

To be afflicted with this condition

It's a bit of an inconvenience

But to sort it, I'm on a mission

Suzy went grey at thirty-six

Dee was just behind at thirty-nine

I suppose 'cause I've lasted to forty-two

I ought to be grateful and shouldn't whine

It's a whole new area of fashion

In which I now find myself

Highlights, low lights, go dark, go light

Such decisions ..... all on one shelf

21. GOLF

Do you think the majority of

Men who regularly play golf

Are named Herbert, James, Toby

Hector, Rupert or Rudolf?

They play for hour upon hour

In trousers checked and shirts pink

It must give their female companions

Plenty of time to think

What is this all about?

Does he care that much about me ?

Does he consider my feelings

As he walks up to the eleventh tee ?

Does he have empathy

Does he have a heart or a soul ?

Am I absent from his conversation

Over G & T's at the nineteenth hole ?

22. WE'RE RUBBISH AT FOREIGN LANGUAGES

Us English are rubbish at languages

In Paris we speak sort of Franglais

But if asked to speak French properly

We exclaim "Can't do that – no way !"

We sometimes have a go at this skill

But all we do is stammer and stutter

While Monsieur or Herr or Signor tries

To work out, "What did he just mutter ?"

We think we're cosmopolitan

We think we're international

But our awful attempts at global interaction

Are illogical, they're just not rational

Why can't we cope with other tongues

The way the World has managed with our own ?

Is it because we think we don't have to

Or is it just that we're lazy bones ?

23. MEN AT FOOTBALL MATCHES

There's a ritual for men at football matches

The build-up : a beer or two or three

But ten minutes into the game

They all need the W.C.

They return to their seats and scream

At the referee they groan

And when their striker fails to score

He'll be targeted for a special moan

They shout, they jump up and down

They love to hurl abuse

Spurred on by their alcohol intake

Their tongues vitriolic, too loose

Then they must return home after

And pretend everything's alright

Now it's their partner to face, not the ref

Their conversation swiftly turns 'light'

All week they had toiled at work

Their boss had to be obeyed

The family too had to be considered

And so at the stadium they had paid

For the right to be the one

Dishing out orders, calling the odds

And instead of positive claps and cheers

They chose to be aggressive – silly sods !

24. DON'T SPOIL THE SHIP

'Don't spoil the ship for a ha'peth of tar'

Not sure exactly what that means

Something like 'don't buy cheap detergent

When there's a better one that proper cleans.'

Like a lot of those old phrases

Such as 'Robbing Peter to pay Paul'

Only pensioners use 'em these days

We just don't understand 'em all

I suppose they're all about common-sense

They're about high standards, good quality

In comparison I suppose today's generation

Are all gratification and no responsibility ?

25. RAMSAY

Gordon Ramsay, chef extraordinaire

Lover of swearing on T.V.

A huge problem arising from this

Is kids "eff-ing" from the age of three

His formative years were spent

In Stratford-on-Avon, so quaint

William Shakespeare would be embarrassed

At language which would make an old dame faint

Such skill, such talent, such prowess

Doesn't need to be expressed so badly

Is he so angry or is it for the cameras

Does he have to react so madly ?

I worry about his blood pressure

I hope he's mellowed and calmed down

If anyone treated his nearest like that

I bet he wouldn't half frown !

26. AUDIENCE IN AN ARENA

Don't you feel a little sorry

For an audience inside a huge arena

Used to be cosy, intimate town halls

When the number of people was leaner

Performers would love the closeness

Of their fans right in front of their face

Now they prefer to be aloof and distant

As if from a different, superior race

'Big head' will pretend to include

Each and every one of the 20,000 fans

But before the final song has faded

He'll escape in a fleet of bulletproof vans

Poor blighters in the back row

For this concert they've spent a week's wage

They didn't feel connected or any part of it

All they saw was a dot on the stage

27. CRICKET

It's a funny old game

That most English of pastimes : cricket

All about aiming a small ball

At three vertical sticks, the wicket

It can take all day long

To settle a cricket match

The batsmen are trying to launch the ball

Past the fielders attempting to catch

Whilst the ball is in motion

The two batsmen need to run

Between the two sets of wickets

It's their idea of 'fun'

There's some very unique rules

Antiquated, traditional and old

Very difficult to comprehend

Is that why so few tickets get sold ?

28. MOVE YER MONEY ABOUT

Switch accounts, move yer money

See which bank is best

You could make two pounds extra

Per year in interest

Keep abreast of interest rates

Keep yer eye on the ball

Shuffle yer assets from pillar to post

If you suspect their value might fall

Not sure if I can be bovvered

Seems like a lot of effort and time

It's not like my 'capital' is the size

Of a mountain tricky to climb

Stuff it, I'll take the casual option

I'll risk leaving things be

And for that two quid I might lose

Next year I'll have one less coffee

29. HOMES

'A home is an Englishman's castle'

So the phrase used to say

Textured wallpaper, crisp curtains

Bright windows in the shape of a bay

For most of the modern era it was

Enough to be tidy and neat

But with the advent of D.I.Y.

There's a challenge in every street

Who's got the most luscious carpet

Who's got a tasteful colour scheme

Who's got the shiniest kitchen

Who's bathroom's nothing short of a dream

T.V. shows dictate that not only film stars

Should have en-suite beds and spacious entrance hall

It's everyone's 'right' to have all this

The issue is : how do we pay for it all ?

30. FUNERALS

Don't people say the strangest things

At funerals of the dearly departed

They meet and greet and reminisce

Before the thing has even started

Some of the congregation though

Have tenuous links with the deceased

But they heard about their sad demise

And their curiosity suddenly increased

They joined the event so that they

Could be nosey : "who's missing ? who's here ?"

Jack's looking well but Betty isn't

Good God she looks fragile, oh dear

Then they bump into the next-of-kin

Can't think of appropriate stuff to say

It suddenly dawns on our gatecrashers

Perhaps I should be somewhere else today ?

31. PLENTY OF POEMS ARE POMPOUS

Plenty of poems are pompous

It's a tradition congealed in English blood

We think that if a theme is simple and basic

Then true poets will think it's no good

The rhythm requires a certain pace

The stanzas need to be a certain size

If they don't conform to regulations

The author will be viewed as dumb not wise

The poems are read with a certain lilt

In tones evoking a certain era

You can try to fathom it all out if you like

But after several attempts you're no clearer

That's because you and I are not supposed to

Comprehend it's contentious themes

We can only guess what's going on

In the writer's imagination and dreams

Connoisseurs of poetry though understand it all

They put forward their theories and critique

They like to reason, dispute and argue

What makes a particular poem unique

Poetry groups sit around all-academic

Pedantic, intellectual, aloof

Funny how they allow Larkin the 'F' word

But if any of us use it, we're uncouth

Their heroes are Tennyson, Keats

Hughes, Dylan Thomas and Blake

But to connect such poetry with 'real' life

Our cultured friends cannot make

They want to take the high-brow stance

They want it all to be elitist

They want less-articulate souls to cower

They'd rather us feel defeatist

They probably think that Michael Rosen

Zephaniah, McGough, Cooper Clarke

Are a bit too down to earth

They prefer stuff from 'The Ark'

They like abstract and surreal, not too blunt

They want us to work hard at analysis

But it's difficult, baffling, frustrating

And the confusion becomes a paralysis

Don't they know that words need to speak to **us**

Our feelings, emotions, our soul

Just the same as music, sport and films

It's called humanity, makes us feel whole

Why get small children excited

About poetry only to let them down

Later in life when it gets all serious

With metaphors from an alien town

Much of poetry is an acquired taste

Like a lot of theatre and art

It doesn't seem to know how to relate

It lacks common ground, lacks genuine heart

Doesn't the poetry world concede that

Rap and hip hop sells to millions of fans

It's exciting, relevant, accessible

While poetry sells to a few asthetes and fancy-dans

And why does a lot of poetry

Lean towards a privileged 10 per cent

When surely rhyme should be fun

Words for everyone were meant

32. 14'S A HORRIBLE AGE

14's a horrible age to be

You're only allowed in a youth club

But if it were up to you and your friends

There'd be room for teenagers at the pub

You might have a boyfriend or girlfriend

But you're not sure what you're supposed to do

You're too young to smoke, drink or vote

And your life experiences are still quite few

At family get-togethers it's you

Who gets sat next to young girls and boys

You've got nothing at all to say to them

And what they say to you is pure noise

You begin to take interest in music and fashion

But with only pocket money and no wage

You'll make no significant purchases

Yes 14's a horrible age

33. CAR MECHANICS

Car mechanics, like a lot of tradesmen,

Have a habit of berating rival guys

They'll claim your car will not be cared for

At "that other garage" which always spins "lies"

Their own form, of course, is exemplary

And the parts they use are bona fide

But 'rival garage' is so unprofessional

Their obvious shoddy workmanship cannot hide

They'll claim that other mechanics

For the chance to work 'here' would kill

Then they blind you with technical terms

And then hope you won't query the bill

34. OBAMA

What a build-up, what suspense

What hysteria, what drama

Leading up to the voting in of

President Barack Obama

Middle-aged male billionaires

Were suddenly out of favour

It was the dawn of a new era

With new choices, a new flavour

He could have earned a fortune

As a lawyer alongside big corporates

Instead worked for a modest income

Helping Chicago's less-than-fortunates

Even JFK and Clinton had problems with trying

To be everyone's favourite Democrat

Barack's a soul music and basketball fan

So obviously no privileged brat

Father of two daughters

Brings empathy, has to be humane

Someone able to share public tears

Suggests a common touch, not too vain

Being leader of the Western world

Means occasionally issuing a threat

But through considered astute diplomacy

Avoids conflict, that's smart – not wet

Martin Luther King's vision no longer seems

Such an impossible mountain to climb

But the Obama factor perhaps

Won't occur again in our lifetime

35. QUIZ CHEATS

There's a quiz at the pub tonight

You're all welcome to participate

All sorts of questions, sports, music, trivia

You can enter in teams of 4, 6 or 8

We carefully choose our squad

Uncle Eric's good at history, Maggie at food

I'm O.K. at recognising a 'pop' tune

A couple of drinks, we'll be in the mood

Then it slowly dawns on us

Some teams – using phones – are on the 'Net

They're cheating in front of our eyes

Our night out, we start to regret

Why doesn't someone stop them ?

Why not put in a formal complaint ?

We want a fair competition

And this farce certainly ain't !

36. THEN THE ALARM CLOCK WENT OFF

Today I'll be the beacon of the office

Nobody at all will scoff

Everyone's gonna be impressed with me

Then the alarm clock went off

Yesterday I didn't feel too good

In fact I had a cough

But today I'll be invigorated

Then the alarm clock went off

That 'stuck-up' supervisor in Accounts

Today he won't act like a toff

He'll be polite respectful and warm

Then the alarm clock went off

37. HOME TOWN

Your home town stays with you always

No matter where you end up living

Relatives of your own and your friends

Always seemed to be readily giving

Whether time, help, assistance

Their benevolence seemed to have no end

And it seemed that – you - to any house nearby

Your mother would happily send

Lots of innocence, laughs, growing

The sounds and smells all familiar

No-one particularly superior or 'better'

Everyone just seemed, well, similar

Your home town stays with you always

No matter how far you end up apart

Right now there'll be new groups of youngsters

All embarking on their own 'home town' start

38. WHAT'S IT LIKE BEING PERFECT ?

It must be a huge burden being perfect

Everyone else is wrong but you're always right

Everyone else's opinions too narrow or broad

But your's are insightful, informative and bright

Everyone else is just being tedious

They're over-emotional, too subjective

Meanwhile your views are based on sound judgement

They're reasoned, intuitive and objective

Everyone else is just being traditional

Or alternatively too modern and fashionable

Meanwhile you are being balanced and able to

Account for every angle fathomable

What the hell is it like being perfect ?

I know I'll never make it to the top

But I'll tell you something you're not so good at

At being liked you're an absolute flop !

39. WHEN I WERE A LAD (2046 A.D.)

It's New Year's Eve 2099

The 22nd century is quite close now

Kids today don't know they're born

With my grandson I just had a row

I told him that our generation

Were a considerate lot

We would share <u>all</u> our drugs

Whether it be hard liquor, crack or pot

We ate sensibly and healthily

At K.F.Cee, B.King, P.Hut, Mac-a-Dee

And would only shout abuse at teachers

If 'Sir' or 'Miss' first made us angry

Those of us who worked put in

A gruelling four hour shift of graft

When I told this to grandson he said

"You daft buggers" and just laughed

40. TAKING UP SPACE AT THE BAR

"That's two beers ..... er ......over here !"

It's a problem when you're getting a drink

If someone's sitting at the bar

You can't get through, you're on the brink

Of thinking "What a dumb obstruction

He knows he's in the way"

But he ain't budging for anyone

'Cause he's a regular – "calls in every day"

Listen mate, not all of us can

Make it here as consistently – so

Allow us 'part-time drinkers'

To order refreshment – please let it flow !

41. HEROES OF '66

I was only seven so cannot

Judge the significance of that day

When we were soccer champs of the World

The "Numero uno's" we were allowed to say

Of course I've seen all the footage

Have seen the clips, the films, <u>that</u> goal

You know, the one where Geoff rips the net off

It causes a shiver in your soul

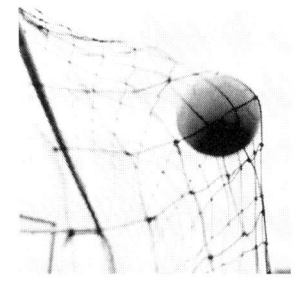

Who were the heroes on that glorious day ?

Banksie, goalkeeping legend at Stoke

Epitomised the class throughout the team

So humble, modest, a right decent bloke

The Geordie brothers, Robert and Jack

The pride of east London, Bobby Moore

A shame my personal hero didn't make the final

Jimmy Greaves, surely a goal he'd have scored

Little Alan Ball, heart of a giant

And gentleman Sir Alf running the show

Might it happen again in our lifetime ?

Always possible but Alex Ferguson says "no" !

42. FIRST JOB

You're hopeless in your 'first job'

Sweet sixteen years of age and not a clue

You know you're supposed to revere the Boss

He'll never be 'Bob' – "it's Mr. Watts to you"

No-one explains anything properly

They all know what to do and where to go

You can't even locate the toilets

And you're tired of packing 20 tiles in a row

All the girls love their cups of tea

The older guys enjoy a 'ciggie – break'

It's a golden ten minute diversion

But for you it's boring...."for f***'s sake"

The day painfully crawls by

An eight hour shift seems at least ten

Decades later you're now doing interesting stuff

The dullness of 'first job' will not be felt again

43. THE TIMES NEWSPAPER

The (London) Times newspaper

First published in 1788

Over two centuries of stories

Views and news for which we don't want to wait

It's the quality of the writing

The journalism respected world-wide

It's what we do well this side of the Atlantic

And why they copy and mimic on the other side

The columnists push the boundaries a little

But always tastefully, respectfully and with humour

There is some gossip and some 'tittle – tattle'

But only if based on evidence, not malicious rumour

I love holding the Times newspaper

How many Times papers are there in the World ?

I love reading the Times newspaper

As the depth of each story's unfurled

44. INSURANCE CLAIMS

How annoying, how frustrating

When an insurance claim is made

That is not based on truth, honesty

But the unscrupulous looking to be paid

They lie about circumstances

They fabricate the evidence

They talk such obvious 'bull-crap'

And do it with oozing confidence

Because of these peoples' naffness

Insurance premiums run sky-high

And continue rising year-on-year

Who picks up the tab ? You and I

45. NORTHERN SOUL

Sometime during the 1960's

A previously unheard sound reached this shore

Across the Atlantic it had travelled

English kids loved it and wanted more

Fanatics occasionally disagree

Whether the 'northern' in this brand so cool

Refers to northern USA (e.g. Detroit)

Or the North of England (e.g. Blackpool)

Russ Winstanley and his team at Wigan Casino

Got the ball rolling for backdrops and spinners

Super-energised feet sliding and high kicks

Natural adrenaline mostly plus a few drugged sinners

All night music and movement, D.J.'s such as

Searling, Roberts, Evison, Curtis, Levine

Live shows by the likes of Major Lance

Half century later, there's still a 'soul scene'

Queen Of Fools, Tainted Love

Ghost In My House, It's Too Late

A few sample titles which prove

What made the times we had simply great

46. IF

If I'd been born at a different time

If I'd been born in a different place

If I'd been born a different gender

Then I might have actually won one race

If I'd been born naturally taller

If I'd been born left-handed not right

If I'd been born with brown hair not blonde

Then I might have actually won one fight

If I'd been born with broader shoulders

If I'd been given a cool name instead of Chris

If I'd been born with thicker skin

Then I'd not worry what readers think of this

If I'd had a...b....c..... instead of x, y and z

If only I'd been allowed 'that' instead of the 'other'

You can make as many excuses as you like but

Your fate is up to you, not your father or your mother

47. WHERE DO SINGLE SOCKS GO ?

After every single laundry wash

There's an issue which rears it's head

Not every single lonely sock

With it's original partner can be wed

What happens to their former mate

Where does that particular sock go ?

Does he/she hide away somewhere

Or does he/she no longer want to show

Perhaps he/she doesn't fancy anymore

Surrounding those smelly toes

Perhaps he/she no longer wants a friend

No longer wants to pair up, who knows ?

Maybe he/she's got a wicked sense of humour

Likes seeing the owner chasing to and fro

All round the kitchen whilst shouting

"Where do single socks go ?"

48. WE'VE BEEN DRAWN AWAY TO NEPTUNE (3046 A.D.)

Got a fair old journey this weekend

After our final training session on the Moon

Our fans have chartered two spaceships because

We've been drawn away to Neptune

We beat Mercury in the previous round

Sweating 'buckets' we were

Mind you our goalscoring winner from that day

Has since, to Pluto, been transferred

When we played Mars there were issues

A pitch invasion by little green men

The three-eyed referee sorted it out though

Splattered them with space gunge then.....

Our wingers showed blistering pace

At 200 miles per hour sprinting like mad

Thank goodness we won that day, if not, the

100 million mile trip home would've been sad

49. COWELL

We're always hearing about the facelifts of Mr. Cowell

But I detect more of a drooping in the jowl

Some say it's time he threw in the towel

That would only cause fans of trivia and piffle to growl

Because they love the style of programmes he makes

Despite the wide range of liberties he takes

Raising emotions which, like some friends, are fakes

As delusion and dreams in losers he awakes

People mock his clothes and his hair

Not that a multi-millionaire would care

What ordinary folk say about him while they stare

At his 'mug' on the box and in tabloids everywhere

Cowell's impact on entertainment can be measured

By the amount of hours he's filled of peoples' leisure

To sum up, because he's given so many so much pleasure

We should leave him alone, he's a national treasure !

Home is where the heart is

That's true for the majority of folk

Ask an English potter where he's from

There's an excellent chance he'll say "Stoke"

The abundance of coal and clay

Brought jobs a'plenty for the people

The master of ceramics, Josiah Wedgwood

Is buried near to Stoke Minster steeple

Branded a genius of science and trade

He was followed by Doulton, Minton, Spode

Midwinter, Wood, Moorcroft, Myott

Their affluence bought many fancy abode

Go to the Gladstone pottery museum

And see how it all used to be made

Then try the Burleigh factory near Burslem

A recent visit by Prince Charles was made

Emma Bridgewater has pots in Harrods

A contemporary Clarice Cliffe-type is she

There's a modern visitor centre at Wedgwoods

A few miles South of the city

But we're not just about ceramic genius

There was Reginald Mitchell master engineer

Without his design of the Spitfire plane

Britain's air dominance would not have been clear

Acclaimed local writer Arnold Bennett

Anna of the Five Towns he penned

Our traditional delicacy the 'oatcake'

Stoke ex-pats miss 'em, they request "please send"

It's perhaps best to not focus too much

On local lad, Captain Smith's, efforts at sea

Although I think he's been forgiven now

'Cause up sprung the Titanic brewery

Sir Stanley Matthews the wizard of dribble

An F.A. Cup final named after him

He'd run to work from Hanley to Stoke

'Super-fit', no need for the gym

Singer and entertainer Jackie Trent

Wrote the theme tune 'Neighbours' for Aussie T.V.

Also the 1972 footy song 'We'll be With You'

As Stoke City made their way to Wembley

We were at the cutting – edge of nightlife

Top class cabaret at Jollees, dancing in The Place

Top Rank, Heavy Steam Machine, the legendary Torch

Later, raves at Shelley's, the Void, proved we kept pace

In the 70's our version of 'Posh and Becks'

Was Anthea Turner and Bruno Brookes

At the time we developed soccer stars

Such as Lee Chapman, Adrian Heath, Garth Crooks

Robbie Williams, global music star

Supporter of Port Vale's football team

They produced Mark Chamberlain, international

Son Alex at Arsenal currently 'lives the dream'

Nick Hancock, T.V. host of 'They Think It's All Over'

Neil Morrisey from 'Men Behaving Badly'

Dominic Cork, once England's main cricket bowler

Phil Taylor picks up World darts trophies gladly

A quarter of a million people

Still live amongst the industrial past

But the heavy manufacturing has largely vanished

So we're having to adapt to new ways fast

John Caudwell and his phones made a billion

The Coates family too, through gaming on the 'Net

With such abundance of entrepreneurialism

There's hope for the future of the Potteries yet

Printed in Great Britain
by Amazon.co.uk, Ltd.,
Marston Gate.